Page |

Page Fright
CAROL BATTON

THE BAD PRESS

Published in 2000
by The Bad Press,
PO Box 76,
Manchester, M21 8HJ.
www.thebadpress.co.uk

ISBN 1 903160 00 6

1 3 5 7 9 2 4 6 8

All rights reserved.
Copyright Carol Batton 2000
but individual poems may be copied
if not for financial or commercial gain.
A CIP catalogue record for this book
is available from The British Library.
Author as a child circa 1960,
Author circa 1997,
Copyright Carol Batton.
Illustrations by Leslie Dicken.
Book designed by Robert Cochrane.
Grateful thanks to Gary Parkinson.

Printed by
The Arc and Throstle Press Limited,
Nanholme Mill, Shaw Wood Road,
Todmorden, Lancs, OL14 6DA.

ACKNOWLEDGEMENTS
'I've Seen Darker'
previously appeared in 'Rialto' magazine.
'The Tea Break' & 'Love Sonnet,'
previously appeared in 'The Big Issue.'
'Born' and 'Too Sad To Kill Myself'
appeared in 'Thoroughly Psychiatric'
a pamphlet published privately in 1995.

CONTENTS

THE CHESTNUT TREE	09
VERSE ORPHANS	10
GENETIC	11
BORN	12
I'D RATHER	13
TOMATO	14
AFTERMATH	15
DRUG SELLING	16
THOUGHT ON THOUGHTS	17
WEED	18
CONFETTI	19
MY LITTLE ANGRY PEN	20
BROWN	21
SOME	22
I THOUGHT	23
SUN BLOCK	24
IT SITS	25
MY POETRY	26
FREE LEGAL TRIP	27
I'VE SEEN DARKER	28
THE AFFECT	29
ANSWERS?	30
FOX	31
DAY DAWNS	32
THE TEA BREAK	33
UNCERTAIN	34
A POET IS...	35

SURPRISING	36
TOO SAD TO KILL MYSELF	37
CONKERS	38
TREES COME BACK TO LIFE IN WINTER	39
GOD LETS BEGGARS BEG	41
FROST	42
GERM	43
LOVE SONNET	44
SYMPATHY	45
DISABLED	46
BEE-ING	47
JANUARY	49
WINTER FLOWERING CHERRY TREE	50
TIME	51
LIKE	53
BELIEF	54
HOMOPHOBIA CAN CURE	55
SPECIAL SUPPORT	56
AIR FORCE MISSION STATEMENT	57
LIFE IS LIKE	58
THE COUNSELLING ENCOUNTER	59
WIND	60
OH! WHAT A LIFE	61
KEY	62
A LIFETIME IS FOREVER	63
OCEAN	64

For My Mum,
Sonia
who wrote, me

"Anyone who cannot cope with life while he is alive needs one hand to ward off a little his despair over his fate... but with his other hand he can jot down what he sees among the ruins, for he sees different and more things than the others; after all he is dead in his own lifetime and the real survivor."

FRANZ KAFKA

THE CHESTNUT TREE

In May,
HE shoots out pollen flowers,
In Autumn, *SHE*, has conkers!
Can a tree now change its sex?
Or am I going bonkers?

VERSE ORPHANS

I sowed a thousand seeds of verse,
I was mother, I was nurse,
and even if I leave them now,
the verses they will surely grow?

I cast a hundred, thousand words,
(Well slightly less, but this is verse),
And know not yet, if blessed or cursed,
Was the effort of that verse.

It's likely only when I'm dead,
That whether they're that good, is said.

It matters not if I succeed,
To think I will, is all I need.

GENETIC

The plant is genetically
engineered to resist the
new super-duper weedkiller;
I'm not.

BORN

Born of a sad too sad for tears,
Bequeathed of a crying that seemed
to last years,
Beset on all sides
by sorrow and fears.

Two days later a poem appears.

I'D RATHER

I'd rather be alone
with a schizophrenic,
than a psychiatrist.

TOMATO

My grandma was a tomato.
My grandfather was a tomato.

But in between
they've added a gene,
and now I'm a bastard,
    soya bean.

AFTERMATH

The poet's path,
is to write about
the aftermath.

There are no,
preventive poets.

DRUG SELLING

Drug pushers from the Drug firms
Make sure, drug use is long term.
Drug pushers from the drug firms,
Don't say, everything, they know and learn.
Rather like a politician -
They lie, to get a good return.

Drug dealers from the Drug firms,
They say, "These make you well",
Drug dealers from the Drug firms...
They legalise hell.

THOUGHT ON THOUGHTS

Your greatest fear
may never come;

It may never, have ever,
been likely even;

For little thoughts,
When given room,
Are bound to lend
Themselves to doom.

WEED

I'm a weed, disabled,
I'm a seed; potential,
I'm a deed, of kindness,
And sometimes, I'm essential.

Even though I'm mad,
Even though I'm mental,
There are moments in my life,
When I'm influential.

CONFETTI

The confetti swirled
along the street,
and the wedding blew away.

MY LITTLE ANGRY PEN

My little angry pen,
Is doing it again,
I've taken it to bed with me,
(No, it is not cuddly),
But fights for justice
By my side,
Revealing things they try to hide.

BROWN

Brown hair,
Brown eyes.
I might be plain;
But I match.

SOME

Some of us are deciduous,
And nearly die in winter.

I THOUGHT

I thought I'd left my sadness,
At the house I'd left behind,
But someone, somewhere, goofed,
And went and packed my mind.

SUN BLOCK

I use a 90% sun block
I got from Oxfam.

No pollutant chemicals in these,
they are called sleeves.

IT SITS

Real desperation
Doesn't ask...
It sits there,
despairing,
sits there;
just staring.

MY POETRY

My poetry is the fruit of my pain,
I hope I don't go bearing fruit again.

FREE LEGAL TRIP

"I'm dizzy and tripping,
 Light-headed and spaced-out."

"What have you taken?"

"My glasses off."

I'VE SEEN DARKER

Dark cloud.
But I've seen darker,
I've seen days
Where there's no light at all.

A little rain,
But I've seen wetter,
I've seen the places
Where the floods take all.

THE AFFECT

The affect of a plectrum upon a kazoo,
is limited, as there is nowt it can do.

ANSWERS?

In Summer the trees have answers;
With answers one can be content.

In Winter the trees have questions -
Unanswered...
About where the summer went.

FOX

They asked the fox to confirm it is vermin...
It replied,
"You eat chicken, too."

DAY DAWNS

Day dawns,
Dusk descends;
Time breaks
More than it mends.

THE TEA BREAK

The cigarette was all she had,
The pills themselves had made her mad,
The medicine had made her sad,
The cigarette was all she had.

The cup of tea was all she had,
The pills had made her very bad,
The medicine had made her sad,
The cup of tea was all she had.

She smoked the cig.
She drank the tea.
And then returned
to ward number three.

UNCERTAIN

I'm the expert on me,
I expect.
But I'm full of regret,
and alone,
and forget.

A POET IS...

A poet is someone
who loves trees -

and prefers paper.

SURPRISING

It is surprising how unsuicidal
one suddenly becomes
when a psychopath enters.

TOO SAD TO KILL MYSELF

On major 'tranquillisers'
I don't kill myself.
I can't do anything at all.

CONKERS

This is the anomaly,
Each age plays with the
seed of tree,
And yet the tree don't cease
to be,
This is the anomaly.

TREES COME BACK TO LIFE IN WINTER

Among the greenery, I can see,
Stark reality,
Black, clawing branches,
Still extant in Winter;
Always there, though hidden in Summer,
Really, where, reality is inside...
Deeper meanings; moanings of Despair,
Inside the tree - Black is there!
Soft matt leaves, mass alive -
Dead wood twigs, are what survive!
Living leaves - the soft screens of Summer;
Twisting wood, harsh screams of Winter.
Though something, shows, of the harsh within,
Yet greenness stirs, and falls in the wind.
The soft leaves go and leave the tree.
It's the bark that endures, on the hard of the tree,
And the twig that lasts for eternity.

Despair endures in our heart;
Towards compassion.
Passion falls in Autumn, wood will always be,
The product of life's hardship,
That lasts for Eternity.
Life lingers on leaves for a year,
But wood expands with time;

In Summer strength unknown beneath,
In winter trees survive the wind.
It's wood as is useful to man;
it's hardness does what it can.

Though leaves are good.
(They cool the heart)
It's your adversity that judges you,
What you make of your Winters,
That merits the true,
The time spent in Sorrow,
Yet still being kind;
Is like the wood that is left behind.

But think not of the leaves that
will leave the tree.
When it's Winter and you still see
Tree,
That is the Strength of Eternity.

GOD LETS BEGGARS BEG...

If God lets beggars beg,
Why can't the City Council?

FROST

The frost grew last night,
The sunlight failed to cease,
The beauty of the sight,
Which will I feel, increase.

The sunlight crept,
with slow, quiet heat,
The green seeped back
to the earth,
The faint heart-heat beat
down in parts...
In others, frost, kept birth.

The day became the night again,
The pain was merely the cold.
The frost it gained in might again,
And might nearly live to grow old.

GERM

Germ - like a worm!
Making my soul infirm.
Learn to remember to try to succeed -
And failure follows in haunting defeat.
And life revolves and all recedes.
And life goes on, but limps and bleeds -
Can't meet anybody's needs.

LOVE SONNET

The man I love has left
this place today...
He's gone from me -
He's very far away.
When I think of him
My mind increases pace;
I think of him all night,
and wonder all the day.

I play my mind on his face
whenever I may.
I visualise him all the time,
each day.
I seek him out, and that
expectantly.
I taste him through my life,
and have to say...

Yet I feel O.K., yet I feel O.K...
I see him in my mind all day,
But by next year, it will be
hard to say,
But I'll send him a card, maybe.

Saying I still think and seek,
But now it's only once a week.

SYMPATHY

"There are people
 worse off than you,"
she said to me;

Trying to cheer me up,
Increasing my misery.

CREATOR

God is disabled -
He is incorporeal,
He has no body.
Somebody must do everything for him.
God, the Creator of the Universe, is disabled.

BEE-ING

Listen you Dandelions!
Don't try to be daisies. Don't try to be tall like the trees.
Did some of you try to be pink? Be content - be yellow.
It is not failure if you are not a pink Dandelion.
Be the flowers you were meant to be...
but learn from others,
learn from the thin grass
and recover from life's blows,
even from trampling boots,
all is not lost if you remember
you have roots.

Live each summer for itself.
Let it be a beautiful summer that lasts
right up to the second frost.
And in winter go underground and grow;
don't just wait.
You don't have to sing
at the very first day of sun,
but by autumn try to have flowered
at least once.

Wait for the friendly little flies.
Take your turn for the sun to find your spot.
Some colours are unlikely,
others impossible, (probably.)
Much can be achieved in

a short flowering season for which
we have waited all winter.
At *any* time there may appear opportunities.
Take credit for having flowered when you could.
(Remember some other year)
and add it to your contentment.

It isn't always as easy to be a flower
as the Trees think it is.
Life is a lot of waiting;
things happen slowly.
We do it for the seeds,
we all know that.
No two flowers are ever the same.
Every Dandelion matters! Trust all.
Recognise that we are all flowers, together,
even the Trees are 'sort of flowers'.

Talk flowers, try to talk.
Stop looking at each other askance.
We are all insecure.
Speak to each other.
Communicate your plight.
Share your doubts.
Talk and tell of truth;
It will fill all that waiting,
with meaning.

by Carol Batton Chrysanthemum

JANUARY

I want to go to summer,
I want to get away,
I want to go to summer -
Every bloody day.

WINTER FLOWERING CHERRY TREE

The cherry that can't
wait for spring -
it gave December everything;
Amid the frozen, shopping days,
It told the truth
of other ways.

TIME

Time may not offer the 'Opportunity'
you want it to offer...
Nevertheless it is yours,
to do with, or to be in.
Time for crying should also be valid for you.
It doesn't matter if there is failure -
it doesn't fail if you survive.
It doesn't fail, it is part of the path,
alongside which are some flowers;
It is path.

The path is O.K. if you say it is O.K.
You are the same you
in successful times, and failed times -

You are true to limitation in both.

There is no going astray when opportunity is limited -
and even the astray bits - can become valuable path,
even if one does not know it;
only death is pathless.

Trust that there could soon be flowers;
paths are like that - flowery in parts.
Find flowers where there is dust and mud.

Path is path when path is muddy

for miles and miles either side -
from mud to mud is equally muddy;
straying is path, staying is path,
choice is path, lack of choice is path.
To say "This is not path",
destroys the flowers and the music.

Time is a harsh master - befriend it;
go at the speed of your want and need.
Own it, claim it all, even the boredom -
Own it until it stops hurting you.
Time is plentiful - don't regret it,
and one week spent befriending yourself,
is only one of 2,500 weeks.

Build when the building is there to be done.
Don't berate yourself for not building
when there are no bricks;
and it is not always obvious
when there are no bricks.

You will regret some - that is par for the path -
follow Tao, don't die, explore doubt, allow doubt,
follow path, follow will, follow whim.

Time is the longest thing in your life.
May God go with you.
May you answer for need, not duty.
May you try to grow, towards that beauty,
below knowledge, near to love.

LIKE

I like sunshine,
I like springtime,
I like walking,
I like talking,
I like eating,
I like thinking,
I like the moon,
I like the sun,
I like all this,
because I love someone.

BELIEF

Belief can make one happy,
And I would rather be,
In fact, myself, quite miserable,
With a truer reality.

HOMOPHOBIA CAN CURE

Homophobia can cure
Arthritis and Depression,
Or is it Homeopathy,
I should mention?

SPECIAL SUPPORT

There should be Special Support
for us straight women...
Imagine being sexually orientated
towards straight men...
I prefer them gay,
But men who are straight
are my destiny.

AIR FORCE MISSION STATEMENT

At 500 miles per hour
I've located my target.

It's square,
(or maybe rectangular?)

I can't tell from the air.

LIFE IS LIKE...

Life is like a game of Chess...
There is usually a possible move
one has not seen yet.

THE COUNSELLING ENCOUNTER

He asked.
He listened.

He felt full Empathy.

But I never knew,
He never told me so.

WIND

Wind - I did not know.
Wind - I did not know
that there were still leaves.
Wind - There are no leaves now...

And where oppression blows its blast,
It's afterwards we ask.
of the lost.

OH! WHAT A LIFE

Oh! What a life -
I don't know what I'm doing,
I feel like a coffee,
but there's only tea brewing.

KEY

She thought it was the key
to University.
It said, 'Yale.'

A LIFETIME IS FOREVER

Many is the time,
I've thought time,
would never pass.
But it always does,
it always has
and I don't know how
(Before it does),
to make it pass.

A lifetime was forever
and has gone
as if it never was.

OCEAN

The ocean is leaking into the sky,
which can't hold the water,
and has to cry.